RETURN TO OPEN WATER

PREVIOUS BOOKS
BY HAROLD RHENISCH

POETRY

Winter, 1982
Eleusis, 1986
A Delicate Fire, 1989
Dancing with My Daughter, 1993
Iodine, 1994
Taking the Breath Away, 1998
The Blue Mouth of Morning, 1998
Fusion, 1999
Free Will, 2004
Living Will, 2005

POETRY CHAPBOOKS

In the Presence of Ghosts, 1993
Kazoo: The Psalm at the End of the Song, 1998
On the Couch of Dr. Daydream, 2001

NONFICTION

Out of the Interior: the Lost Country, 1993
Tom Thomson's Shack, 2000
Winging Home: A Palette of Birds, 2006
The Wolves at Evelyn: Journeys Through a Dark Century, 2006

FICTION

Carnival, 2000

TRANSLATIONS

Peyote, or My Friend the Indian, by Stefan Schütz, 2001

EDITIONS

Linda Rogers: Essays on Her Work, 2004
Facing the Light, by Robin Skelton, 2006
In This Poem I Am: The Selected Poetry of Robin Skelton, 2007

return to
open water

POEMS NEW & SELECTED

Harold Rhenisch

RONSDALE PRESS

RETURN TO OPEN WATER
Copyright © 2007 Harold Rhenisch

RONSDALE PRESS
3350 West 21st Avenue
Vancouver, B.C., Canada V6S 1G7
www.ronsdalepress.com

Typesetting: Julie Cochrane, in New Baskerville 11 pt on 13.5
Cover Design: Julie Cochrane
Cover Art: Serdar Yagei, "Steps to the Sea"
Paper: Ancient Forest Friendly "Silva" — 100% post-consumer waste, totally
    chlorine-free and acid-free

Ronsdale Press wishes to thank the following for their support of its publishing program: the Canada Council for the Arts, the Government of Canada through the Book Publishing Industry Development Program (BPIDP), and the Province of British Columbia through the Book Publishing Tax Credit Program and the British Columbia Arts Council for their support of its publishing program.

Library and Archives Canada Cataloguing in Publication

Rhenisch, Harold, 1958–
    Return to open water: new & selected poems / Harold Rhenisch.

ISBN 978-1-55380-050-7

    I. Title.

PS8585.H54R48 2007   C811'.54   C2007-902435-1

At Ronsdale Press we are committed to protecting the environment. To this end we are working with Markets Initiative (www.oldgrowthfree.com) and printers to phase out our use of paper produced from ancient forests. This book is one step towards that goal.

Printed in Canada by Marquis Book Printing Inc.

CONTENTS

The Sacred Years

—

The Farming Years

—

The Lyrical Years

—

ACKNOWLEDGEMENTS

"Words in January" and "The Mill" first appeared in *Winter*, and are printed here with the kind permission of Sono Nis Press.

Selections from "Songs for the Moon" first appeared in a slightly different form in *Eleusis*, and are printed here with the kind permission of Sono Nis Press.

"Evelyn, B.C., 1947," and a slightly different version of "The Koan" first appeared in *A Delicate Fire*, and are printed here with the kind permission of Sono Nis Press.

"Dancing with My Daughter," "A Grammar," "Water," and "Drawing Hands" first appeared in *Dancing With My Daughter*, and are printed here with the kind permission of Sono Nis Press.

"Hymn for Small Engine Repair," "Graceland," "The Song of Our Lord, or There Ain't No Cure for Love," and "The Prodigal Son II: A Steven Spielberg, Francis Ford Coppolla Co-Production" first appeared in *Iodine* (Wolsak & Wynn).

"What to Do When You See Pat Lane's U-Haul Broken Down at Standing Rock," "Moving a Greenhouse," "Sharing the Mouth of the Wind Among Friends and Consecrants," "The City Without Angels," "The City of Witches," "A Private Screening," and "The Fish," first appeared in *Taking the Breath Away* (Ronsdale Press).

"Home on the Range," "Paradise Found," "The Scent of the Earth," "Plato's Penance," "Return to Open Water," "The Renaissance Confessional Boxes," "The City is Famous for Libraries and Houses of Music," and "The Message" first appeared in *The Blue Mouth of Morning*, and are printed here with the kind permission of Oolichan Books.

"Shy Deer," "Raking Gravel," "Birdsong," and "The Kingfisher" first appeared in *Fusion*, and are printed here with the kind permission of Exile Editions.

"Telling the Truth," "*from* The Uncollected Sonnets of Mr. W.S., Translated from the English," "Without a Clue," "Iago's Version," "Oh What Fools These Mortals Be," "Gertrude's Version," "Desdemona's Wedding," and "Grief," first appeared in *Free Will* (Ronsdale Press).

"Tao Hill" first appeared in *ARC*, and received the 2004 *ARC* Poem of the Year Prize.

"Stirk" first appeared in *Chiaroscuro*.

for Diane

The Sacred Years

—

WINTER (1978–1980)

ELEUSIS (1981–1985)

IODINE (1987–1990)

Words in January

Dusk is the darkest time of the year.
Clouds squeeze in now
fuming with night and snow
and hasten on;
caught alone at dusk, a man
must stop himself
and wait to hear his blood
or he will be lost
in the new year.
I settle, slowly,
into a bed of old fruit and leaves
and wait for the bear
to rumble over this abandoned orchard,
his yellow eyes flashing,
lick himself, and rumble on,
his nails clattering.

Every year I leave on a journey
and every winter
I pause here a while
and leave in the morning,
stiff and cursing,
into a sky of blood.
I don't know why I come.

Last night the bear raked the sky
into tatters of milk
and soil.
I have no answers:
I can only look up into clarity or clouds
and wonder.
Moving once and lost
I discovered these bent trees

black with age and fruit
and I come here, alone.
I don't know why I come.
I walk in the tumbling dusk
and lean against a crumbling velvet limb
in the dark of winter
because my eyes hurt
and I can hardly breathe.
But I don't know why I come.
I watch — and wait for days —
and shiver.

Last year I watched entire histories
move on to newer ground,
swarms of celebrants running down,
their hair full of pine cones
and milk, from the mountains.
I watch the earth now.
Look how the blackbird
tears at the brown, hanging skin
of an old sweet apple,
and sways, and sings —
and the last red leaf clatters
against a black limb.
Look how the stars come in,
trembling,
shaking out their hair
into streams of light.
They weave the light back in
with dark arms.
At times I have heard
them sing,
softly,
without any words at all.

It's hard to speak in this darkness.
It's better to walk,
your blood like wet leaves —
to walk hard
and to keep on walking
until you hear trees above you
and you can lie down.

In the winter darkness
after the rains at dusk
the black trees are born
in the winds and sway,
and tremble,
troubled and very old.
One can only say they thrive.
And do we thrive like that?
One can only say we do.
If I speak to you at all, remember:
my voice is coming from the darkness:
it has only one
direction,
it knows nothing
of the light.
If I carry anything,
it is the smell of rotted fruit,
of mildewed leaves and clattering grass
I carry,
and that is a smell
that makes a man stay awake for a year
and shake in the wind.

The Mill

I

In a fluid darkness
bent by stars,
all direct lines
are curves of stone
cracking on the river bottom,
shudders of light
learning wetness, flesh,
stone turned inward
to learn the hardness inside stone.

I held this truth once.
Do you want truth?
Myself, I have stopped
asking for truth
but ask for simplicity,
and it confounds me.

We fall, straight, hard,
into the sun of where we've been,
and come out flesh,
not space, but yielding stone: earth.
It is a flying leap.

I have walked
the great gravel bars;
I have lain in the black furrows
as the cold came up;
I have watched the dusk
come up, stood silent
at the first shivering star.

My year is a restless
pushing at skin
until I can lie
on the frozen earth;
for spring also must learn
from where it comes,
another truth.

    II

Beside me runs the river,
its flow cloudy with loess.
I sit on sand and stones
and begin again.
I reach to learn anything,
to learn why we tremble
in the pale light,
the air too clear —
and yet too murky
for me to see or hear more
than my own earth.

How far have we come or gone?
It is cold.
I throw a stone into the current.
It drifts.
What is time to us?
We are time,
the most difficult answer.

First star of night,
millwheel, I have come
to learn something from myself,
or — I have come here
to forget myself again.
Star, we have gone the different ways

of differing flesh
and yet still must speak
to one another.
There is nothing else.
We have come through
another year and know even less.
We have forgotten
our deepest names.

The leaf falls, the body rots,
the moments end.
This is not a truth
but something every man
must stand against
in his own time.
Hard knowledge:
only love brings life
to fallow flesh.
Such simplicity confounds me.

from Songs For The Moon

fifth song

The sun is a white glare
glancing off a crow's blue wing feathers,

a tongue spinning on the mouth of the sea,
a leaf of fire

flashing up in wind so loud with light
the crows are silent

and shift darkly against the storming sky.

These last few days,

a cool breath behind my back, or,
before my face, a sinking resolve, silence

has been flowing into my day

and now flows over its cupped lips
and back into silence,

black as stones rolling through a river's hands —
but this time bearing away a world.

Your words echo in my ears like seasons
remembered across life,

so many friends gone, their voices loud —
a man calling for me out of death

with words I can remember
only long enough to speak.

I speak the word you would have me speak
and then throw my head sideways, dead —

is that what you wanted — what do you want?
Pull yourself together

and ask me in a language we can share or keep.

I answer whatever voice of yours
can make it through to me;

as water welling
from the cold gravel at your feet:

touch me so I may learn
the fires of leaf and soil

and I will be yours,
not in surrender

but in a form of love
similar to surrender,

surrender dignified,
the silence

of speech at last
pouring from my dark mouth.

sixth song

I speak far ahead of my life,
in a thin sliver of pain

that will not leave.
It is a strength I have failed too often —

it is brutal and sings in the blood
without companion or fear

as all our voices die and our lives go on,
spilling like green air into our cracked mouths:

we drink them down then lean back in our chairs,
refreshed: "So that," we say

as if we retained any balanced, earth-thick thought,
"Is what we meant by dream and knew by time." Well,

it is not. It is our own fear come alive;
it is our lives come to haunt us:

speaking is easy; it's walking
in breath that's hard. It's saying,

OK, I'll be still. All day
I've been too still.

I have forgotten myself into memory;
I am alone with words —

no world around me but silence
behind glass.

Night is a bucket of water
thrown against a window, a fast splash,

spread by time over a long
echoing pulse of light,

my breath pressing against the glass
as I begin to wake into my own drunk air,

light pouring off the window
like waves emptying out of storm,

like a man's life
pouring out of his eyes in sleep —

and then he wakes too suddenly,
saying there is nothing left,

how can you go on with such stillness —
it is then you have to go on.

seventh song

The wind tears me wide,
a fall afternoon of intermittent rain,

leaves gusting off my bones
and scattering through my veins —

words breaking into soil
with the falling sun,

my tongue, twisted dry in my throat,
swallowing itself into thirst

— the taste of windfall apples
that can't be held.

It blows through my veins
in all the noise of leaves;

it corners me in the twisted
root ways of my fingers,

swallowing me into its own earth:
the sun

sprays down through the air,
a voice more full than any human voice.

Rain gusts over it; my breath
blows against it, skittering:

surrender is only folly;
the sun speaks out our time and our swaying,

dancing bodies, leaves
spinning just under the surface

of a cold stream we swim through
in the dark world which is ours to share.

Hymn for Small Engine Repair

As the faller longs for virgin timber

    and the moss crackling underfoot

So do we long for our Lord

and as the pipefitter longs for Saturday

    so he can wake up beside his wife
    and turn over to hold her

    because his skin feels like sheet metal

and his bones like galvanized iron

    so does our god
    long for lightning all night
    and white rain in the morning

so he can watch all the farmers get up
and walk around aimlessly, waiting

    not knowing what to do

with such freedom!

    So does the god of the fouled sparkplug

open up a small engine repair shop
in the weather-beaten garage behind his trailer

    It is perfect!

right down to the "Briggs and Stratton" sign

nailed above the door
and the rusted lawnmowers

    strewn around through the cactus
    and the sagebrush

When I sit down and think on it
I want to weep

    Because when the people start to come

in their nylon-mesh hats with the sun-faded brims
their pickups bouncing over the shale

    and drag their broken machines before him

I want to see him come out
of his dark doorway

    Because I want to see the pity in his eyes

I want to see how he handles it

    when his people return to him

I want to be *there*

Graceland

Our lord

    the carpenter

comes out of the woodwork

    writhing, white, and blind

Wherever there is a nail
and a hammer

    He is there between them

and wherever there is one hour
between the morning and the evening

    that is from neither the pas de deux nor the stilleto

He is there

    with his brace and bit
    and his claw hammer

He loves nothing better than a young woman

    pulling on her panty hose
    her hairbrush in her teeth

Like the Bata Shoe salesman
at Orchard Park Mall in Kelowna
who looks first at a person's feet on introduction
and then only then clasps their hands in his

Praise him!

Oh we adore him!

    May we never be parted
    from the waiting room
    at the Canadian Tire Service Centre
    in Penticton

For he is there
standing on a carhood up on the hydraulic hoist
with a microphone

    dressed in rhinestones

giving his Elvis impression

    Love me Tender!

Love me true!

The Song of Our Lord, or
There Ain't No Cure for Love

Dad
  kick off your hiking boots
  and wash your feet
  in the Similkameen River

that drains the sky through us!

  Because there is a worm
  in every bottle of spring water

Because there is a worm
under every pillow

  Because there is a worm
  in every mouth

and we need a rest!

  You can see everything

but we are only a tired crew
at the end of the nightshift

  walking off into the streets of Moscow
  and beating back the Germans
  with our pipe wrenches and sledgehammers

and we need a rest

You're strong all right

like the yellow floodwaters of the Fraser

but we are just kids, Dad
we like the *National Geographic*

We're tired of books without pictures

We need an afternoon nap!

The Prodigal Son II: A Steven Spielberg, Francis Ford Coppolla Co-Production

When the disciples were walking back to their nets
and their vineyards, the lord revealed himself

to them. He was wearing Calvin Klein jeans
and a $140 Pierre Cardin sweater,

and they bowed down before him in shame.
The lord laughed: "Rise, and go spread the Good News,

that your lord has died, but now he has risen;
Death is a prisoner in his own kingdom;

rejoice! There is no good and no evil —
I have banished them outside of time!

Rejoice and spread the good news!"
The lord spent the rest of the day among them,

sitting under the ashen olives,
drinking their sour wine, laughing. He seemed

more like a brother to them than ever,
and he held each one closely to him in his grasp

when he said good-bye. The disciples carried the word
to every corner of the desert. Everywhere

the people heard it, in all the villages and the small huts
of the shepherds among the rocks,

there was rejoicing, there was good wine spilt,
and much late laughter; many a child was conceived

in the rejoicing; the sounds of the partying
filled the land and the air right up

to the seat of God. He looked down afraid
and troubled for his son, on his walkabout. In the heavens

there was no laughter, for every glance taken in Death's
                                    kingdom
has a life of its own, every

indrawn breath, every exhalation,
every touch of the fingers to stone,

lives on, splits away into its own wind,
its own stars and its own ocean,

and down there in the violent winds
his son was walking incognito,

trying to gather up the pieces that had left him.
He had very little time,

and the penalty if he failed
was total annihilation.

There was no laughter in heaven.
Down on the earth the wind blew across the desert,

and burned as it struck the face
with the hand held across the eyes, to shield them.

The Farming Years
—

A DELICATE FIRE (1980–1989)

DANCING WITH MY DAUGHTER (1986–1993)

TAKING THE BREATH AWAY (1987–1997)

FUSION (1984–1992)

What to Do When You See Pat Lane's U-Haul Broken Down at Standing Rock

Swing open the back doors
and let the horses out.

Sit down on the soft shoulder
and watch them run across the alfalfa
to the river.

They slip among the fern-shadows
of the cottonwoods
and are gone.

Ahh! Can't you smell the knapweed?
Like creosote on the fingers.

As for Pat, brew him a cup of coffee
out of the crushed gravel.
Sweeten it with the sun —
overhead like a quail's egg.

He's been away for too long.

The breakdown was a prophecy.
Why do you think they rent those trucks
so cheap?

How did you think they managed it?

Subsidized industry — that's the Canadian way.

You don't need to say a thing to each other,
just sit there shoulder to shoulder,

as the grass sways in the moon's tides,
and the mountains drift, weightless,

and the stones shudder,
flick their manes, and run.

Moving a Greenhouse

The first weather sign for Rain: Barn.

The other signs: Glass;
Wing;
Shattered seed; sun all day,
with brief showers toward evening,
mauve light through the willows,
a flower spilling out dusk;
a broken flask;

high wind, tattered cirrus.

The weather sign for ash: black knife
of the tongue,

broken jar of the night.

Those signs are the eyes.
Those are the windows.
Those are the laughter
in the fingers
that dance over the Earth's skin,
like a drum
made of petals,
a breath made of bees,
a splinter of the evening breeze
brought across such a distance
it is now a word.

They've placed it under glass.
The people crowd around,
behind ropes.

Art used to be to honour the dead,
by aiding them. *That*
was the hard part of life, to keep it going
without the body,
and, above: the sky,
absolutely clear,
absolutely empty.

This is the weather sign for night:
clouds on the horizon,
men raking the loose soil
under the blighted fruit trees
of their heat-parched gardens,

taking the air in by great mouthfuls:

and within them, slow, giant fish
moving behind their eyes,
pushing their flanks
up against the glass
as they slide by,

breathing, slowly,
under the carbon dioxide skies.

Sharing the Mouth of the Wind
Among Friends and Consecrants

Full moon last night.

The sky a wind looked at on edge.

Damsel flies sitting on the thistles —
the whole field shimmering, blue,
then lifting off, scattered.

Words set out along a fence rail;
kid with a .22: the old need to extend the mind
into the territory of the body.

Without patience, without sorrow,
the edges are wearing off each molecule of water.

Whole world like molten glass,
whole sky like a lung.

The moon dreams me.

The trees tiptoe around us, and flee:
ghosts of insatience.

We lie in the grass side by side,
cold, drenched with dew.

Words like the edge of a file
slid across a knuckle,

like the hundred knives of a saw blade
cutting through the jeans into the knee.

Patience an old myth
gathered from a distant tribe,
and celebrated in the biggest cities.

Rain.

Evelyn, B.C., 1947

When my mother
was a girl
she lived in the shadow
of a glacier

All summer
the wind fell
off the ice
and into her

In winter
the moose
would follow the cows
into the barn
at night

there in the dark
with the great wooden beams
between them
and the frozen
light of the moon
they would stamp
fretfully

In the cabin
of rough-fitted logs
behind the barn
a young girl
would toss
in her sleep

around her
there was an inch
of frost
on the newspaper
of the walls

Sometimes a birch tree
would explode nearby
with the cold
and she would startle
awake

When she walked
to the main house
in the morning
in that dry winter air
that tasted of steel

her feet wrapped in newspaper
inside her gumboots
she would come in
to the thin
dark warmth of the kitchen

Her mother
was training her
not to waste food
and so served to her
the boiled
pig's lung
she had choked on
the night before

and milk
that tasted of cow's breath
and greasy hair

While outside her father
was pulling open
the great doors
of the barn
and the moose
stepped out past him
antlers held proudly
above them

like thoughts frozen
as soon as they hit the air

All the time
there was not a breath of wind
only the cold
slipping off the glacier

and the wolves
slipped through the shadows
between the birch trees
behind the house

thin with hunger
they walked
right on the surface
of the snow.

The Koan

The leaves
that were dry yesterday,
and which drifted
against the front step,
are now wet
and cling to the edge of the concrete:
they have suddenly crossed over the threshold
away from light.

Language too
is much like the building of a house:
once a sentence has been laid down
in the contorted logic,
the rough debit and credit, of the mind,
choking on silence,
the language can move through it at will,
from room to room;
sometimes she can be glimpsed
dropping her clothes
to the floor: her skin
is like the skin of a sapling,
clear.

The leaves are not waiting for a lover,
but they too follow a musical logic —
the music is not important,
how could it be — with nothing to say;
it is arithmetic: however the instruments,
and the variations
within the weed-skeletal trance of the music,
the lengths to which the music
is driven
to escape the patterns of the human mind,

and the sheer sweat
the composer forces into it
to bring it back to human form
before it disappears into clarity
are crucial:

and that is why Mann's *Faust*
is the greatest
of all orchestrated music — a bitter irony,
for it does not exist:
it is not there, and cannot be listened to,
yet we have all heard it,
the dark seduction of a human hell —
like the wet embrace of a temple prostitute,
her lips soft and without tension,
her thighs crusted,
her eyes dark as hate,
like a dog's, and if that music did exist,
we would not be able
to bear it: it would tear us apart.

I was going to go,
in the last half hour of the light,
to Wayne's;
and in the mixed scents of steamed cabbage,
wood dust, garlic, and honey,
ask him for koans,
to bring home
for study; but as I was about to leave,
I saw the mountain, BLACK,
and not an impalpable, transparent blackness
either —
hell, I had been inside
too much today,
and gathered up my daughter,
and went out to rake up leaves,
the light sinking,

palpably,
out of the air.

As I scooped the damp leaves,
with my thick fingers,
out of the cold grass, my daughter
methodically
lifted two lengths of applewood,
their bark rough and torn from the chainsaw,
up onto the steps and then down,
one at a time,
absorbed:

seeing her there
with hardly any light, I felt the whole day
drain out of the air around me,
and bent down to scoop up the last leaves,
my fingers stiff and hard,
the claws of a bird: I had my koan.
Each time you listen to music
it is different music, as each time
it expends itself: that is, perhaps,
the definition of irony;
all that breath poured into a form
that already has unlearnt more
than we have gathered
from its broken breath.

The old man next door laughed
when he first saw them
sprout up through the grass; they were like flowers.
He could not hold back; he spat: "I chopped
that son of a bitch out
two years ago: the thorns
ripped right through the leather of my gloves."
He held out his hands,
and I thought *locusts*! and my blood

tightened in my fingers,
and my wrists went stiff;

and now they are ten feet tall,
a dozen trees,
tender-barked, clustered together,
young girls at the edge of the grass:
it's like those women's magazines
from early this century — one hundred quarto pages
of genteel advertisements, shallow articles
about culture, of all archaic notions,
and a bewildering number of advertisements
selling pianos —

or like those pictures of naked Jewish women
in the pine forests of Poland,
a skiff of half-melted and refrozen snow
under the trees,
the women pale, running, barefoot,
along the edge of a ditch
full of corpses — frozen in that cold,
contorted: who are these women?
They had no strength to scream; that is obvious:
it is a waste of strength to scream:
they were concentrating
on the breath pounding in their lungs
and out through their throats,
their legs weakening,
until they were booted into the ditch,
almost mercifully,
and shot, like rats.

I said to my neighbour
I was going to move the trees
to the back of my garden,
between my garden and the alfalfa
growing there out of the rocks,

and he was pleased;
the balance of the weight
on his legs shifted
completely,
and he was, for a moment,
younger, taller,
and then his spine
curled back on itself
again, and he cleared his throat roughly,
and his eyes darted,
furiously,
as if he did not really understand
what the hell I had meant:

I was putting them there
to drink the wind; that you only
have once chance in this world
to live: what could I tell him?
That there was the clever poet
who concealed the earth
from the world just this year
by talking of three thousand years
of Jewish scholarship, interpretations
and reinterpretations
of the Talmud —
and in each generation
men of the calibre of Einstein and Freud;
that in the face of such humanity
you cannot claim to know anything?

The filbert bush along my fence
blossoms all winter
and gives fruit,
which when dried and cracked
can be eaten
to give the taste of the wood,
the blindness within the root

of the filbert,
the black loneness of the soil;

the apple,
when plucked from a black, wet limb
three days after the first hard frost
that has withered the tomatoes
into their blight, and cupped
with the blossom end to the fingers
in the palm of a man's two hands,
can be cracked in half
to bring to light flesh
that has not before seen light,
which is white,
unblemished,

and there within,
in a star-shaped, fibrous tissue
which is the womb of this tree, a few brown
and bitter seeds:

so too is the mind not only a flower
that can open
and so provide a small bowl
for light,
said Chuang Tzu
after a lifetime of concentration
on concentration,
but is also a seed,

a flower that closes upon itself
and, old and brittle,
its petals withered and scattered,
loses all shape of itself,
so forming a kernel
that can crack the teeth.

The painter
grows into her craft:
she spends a lifetime above the lake,
and so over time learns
or rather relearns —
light, as it pours down over the hills
and lights even the depths of the lake:

yet it is not the mind
that burns within her canvas,
illuminating it
but the thick residue of those years
of the sun pouring over her face;
she is like a block of wood
set aflame: by concentrating the light
through the forms of her art,
she so intensifies it
that she is burnt away:
there is no kernel,
no completion.

Similarly, it is not a useless activity
to page through books
to find the breath of living men,
for you will soon find — your eyes going black
with the realization — that it is a useless activity:
it is better to go out and stand
in the flood-raked,
snapped-off stalks of sandbar willow
below the abandoned bridge
of the Great Northern Railroad
over the mercury shadow
of the Similkameen River
in the wind, your jacket snapping about you,
the whole earth in motion,
and clouds dissipating,
in the force of the wind,

directly into sky: it is a great
industrial construction above you
and blocks out the better part
of the sky, but it is there:
it is best, as Kung said,
to do something in particular.

The prophets of Greece
before the invention of writing,
claimed to have had, while sleeping,
their ears licked out by snakes,
and so were able to hear
the speech of birds;

the koan sets before you
a purpose and the means
to achieve that purpose,
whereas the purpose itself
is to have no purpose,
and to strive to no end,
but to be a receptacle,

and so forces the mind
to snap,
and if there is no kernel there,
it is because it is the world.

Dancing with My Daughter

I have buried myself in the land
that was ours and is lost
and have lived with the cherries
that burst out from the trees
at the nodes of intense pressure
all up and down the limbs.
Now I want to sit among friends.

The body's surface fire
gathers itself into the breast:
dark, bruised bursts of flame,
brought into the animal rage
of the body drinking
inhuman time:

but what can we make out of fire?
Fire? I want to sit among friends,
as the year dies in broken weedstalks
and the pine on the sandbar thunders up
taller than the mountain,
defiant,

and the snow blasts over the dark house.

And for friends I have to look to women
who are wasting away their time,
and men who drink wine
in their gumboots
in the unheated garage,
in celebration of the fire in the shale,
the inexhaustible flame.

We are a people leaving the land,
for the comfort of old songs:
time, strength, soil, light:

old nodes of pressure,
the goddess stepping barefoot
into the god's dance.

I do not know if it was the words
that weakened us,
their community that destroyed
us: beauty, soul, honour, poetry, art,
the old emblems: beauty,
form held in balance, the body
stripped away
from ineffable light, the gulf
of dark; soul,
the mirror of poetry
in the perfect form
of measured time; and honour,
the personal guarantee for death;
that separate poetry from art:

old, banished words,
cheap porcelain down at the junkshop,
old bent tin frames, old dolls
with taped-up arms.

I would like to think the wind is a broom tonight,
cleaning us out, but it is not:
the leaves are sodden and limp,
and empty of light, and will not catch
that cold and leering fire.

In the world without music,
I wanted to sit here tonight to remake this earth
in the image of a balsam root

burning yellow in the green night fields,
with a soft wind spilling through the grass, warm,
the gentle waste breath of ants
in their opium heavens,
not to repeat the old words again,
the terrible old words
of possession and judgement
and power:

meaning, logic, compassion;
truth.

I want to sit here tonight among friends.

In this burning world, this sea of blue stars
smashed across a stone floor,
I have been given a daemon with a lash.
He wants to teach me one thing,
and he wants to teach it to me well:

we have no friends;
we are alone;
there is no shared world;
love, like God, is dead,
pressed flowers between the pages of a book,
Keats' hand caressing our cheeks as we dream,
childhood lilies remembered in old age,
candles, matches of memory,
brief flares in the unending dark. Night
is an idol cast into stone:
there is nothing there.

My five-year-old daughter
dances with me in the kitchen,
laughing, her eyes bright.
That, I have taught her.

It's all I have.

I would like to say
the lash will not reach her,
that as we dance
the imposter's lash will strike my back
and not her face;
that those welts are mine.

I can say it,
but all I have to say it with are these burning words;

and leaves, plastered against the cold ground,
so flat they have lost dimension and mass,
eternal, that belong to none of us,

won't ever shield her from that.

A Grammar

1909. Keremeos.
The first ranches are broken up
into mortgages on hard terms and orchards,
newly planted, that will not pay
before 1919. Irrigation flumes run dry
with bad engineering and the strain of heat
this land no longer knows.
The sage lies withered on the hills.
It is the old story: Kelowna, Peachland, Summerland:
lots sold on the bottom of Okanagan Lake —
the whole lake bottom neatly drawn up
. and sold — sight unseen — to prairie men, new Canadians,
as an escape from cold and a way of life
that never was.

All the old varieties are gone: Snow, Wolf River,
Belle de Boskoop, Maiden's Blush, Cox Orange,
that returned to England, and home, no better than pig-fodder,
and nearly ruined the dream:
Victuals and Drink, Winter Banana, Raspberry Sweet:
all gone, all useless to this land:
flavourless apples, soft punk:
Northern Spy, American Mother, Golden Russet —
that could not bear the heat
and grew tough-skinned: abandoned, and men with them,
in favour of Spartan
(Macintosh X Newtown, Summerland Research Station, 1922),
and Red Delicious (orig. Hawkeye,
Starks Bros. Nurseries, St. Louis Missouri, 1890's) — not
                                        dreams,
but the harsh reality of industry
without market: export, production, wealth: a grammar.

Give those first farmers their due:
I've picked New York Macs
off a tree planted in 1909,
and though I do not wish
to glorify a deadly foolish past,
green as two-day-old hay, they had a flavour
and the scent of earth —
a huge, half-dead snag of a tree —
thirty trees to the acre, to last a lifetime,
unlike the Macspurs I picked earlier in the day,
95% red, 95% Fancy or Better,
money hanging on the trees,
bland and watery,
picked from the ground,
850 trees to the acre,
on rented land, to last ten years —
realities of the production of a product
in oversupply, 1981, East Kelowna —
the product is dreams.

It was called building a country,
and building a life:

we cannot build these things now
except by accident;
that first luxury is gone:
there is no wealth
but what we draw from this soil,
no families in England paying to get us out
from underfoot: we are gone,
lost to the far side of the world:
our wealth is in this soil —
and whether in the trading of dreams
for dollars or for dreams,
the choices are clear.

Water

This is not one of the Sefiroi
that is burning, phosphorescent,
in this dark room — the shape
of the night is showing
through the form of the room —
but the scent that wafts from it
is the scent of hay:
it is a thing of light,
a nest for birds, a jug
that will hold no water:
it is the body.

Mountains and trees are also
thin filaments of light:
the mind, perfectly attuned,
will look through them
and see Nothing — they are
the heavy seedheads of grass
in rain;

as soon as the body steps
out of the door
and the wind moulds itself
exactly to its face, it ceases
to be the body,
but is the threshing floor;

music is continually fighting
to return to its first
note, but no longer has within it
the form of a tree — it can form
the song of a tree, but can put forth no leaves,
gently fingering the light
like angels.

I have just stepped out the back door
into the sky. The light
in the leaves under the apricot trees,
and the light off the water
on those leaves, to hold
the frost from the roots,
is reflecting the sky:
the sun is burning within them —
but cooled, and still.

If you break apart
the sacred geometry of the Sefiroi,
you get no more than a heap
of light on the ground,
that quickly seeps out through the grass
until it is a skin
that so perfectly fits the shape
of leaf-blade and gravel
that it has unlearnt
itself — and all so quickly
that the mind does not see
that it is there, or even
that it was within its hands.

With such visions the body
walks down out of the bush,
dark with rain, smelling of clouds, and simply
to see the light burn up over its face
and to feel the shadows of light
burn down its throat as the door opens,
knocks lightly on the door of the mind
and asks for water. Music too
tends to unlearn itself
when thrown into the grass.

The body sees all, and because
it does not know what to make of it,
and with what it knows
cannot return into the water
the mind has given it
in a white pitcher,
but can drink it,
and so, bitterly, drinks — rain,
and wind through alders, the moon
shivering, a blur — and so
shivers, it dreams;
and those dreams are the mind.

If you break apart
the sacred geometry
of the mind, you get the body:
it smells faintly of a flame.
You can learn much from it,
like water poured down the throat
out of the hands,
directly into the rough woodwind
notes of a tree,
so coarse they seem at first
without relation to water.

Shy Deer

On old trails through the scrub,
following the ridgelines in the starlight,
with the land falling out below,
mountain range upon mountain range,
each a deeper blue than the last,
dropping into fog
and the distant sea,
Basho tried to lose language
in the touch of bamboo and tree
and water. It would not leave.

Today, as I attempt to shake my words off
among the muscat-scented petals of the dog roses,
like a fish leaping into the sky
to shake a flea from under its scales I realize
too that language does not leave,
for it is only the words
that give a sense of their absence. Like Basho,
with no other choice before me
I have gone out to *them*, and have been accepted,
and like Basho I find it no relief: the light
comes in low, a fast wind off Starvation Flats,
catches the rain on its flank
and transforms it instantly
into a platinum fire.

By trying to see through the blue and dancing air,
I have come in the end
only to the simplest necessities:
the river is "river", mountain is "mountain,"
pines are "pines": words I have never heard before,
and have never spoken. The sky
plays over my face. What it says
I hear out of a corner of my words — a quick flash,
like a deer slipping out of a clearing.

Raking Gravel

There is a small green stone in my driveway
that was Picasso once — when he was living
right in the surface layer of his perceptions.
On one side floated the midges and damselflies
of a horsetail-scented dusk, the radioactive,
primal world splitting
from the scum of pine pollen on the belly of the air,
poisonous, impossible to touch;
on the other side, the dark, untouchable shadows,
ten thousand years of condensed mist,
and rain, and the cold-blooded,
unblinking bottom fish. At the middle was Picasso,
in the immeasurably thin skin of light
playing over the water of his retina,
in all the reflected and glowing colours
of trees and houses and clouds
and reeds — casting them back on the sky.

That might be enough for Picasso now,
but for me the lake and trees burn there
only when I watch them from the shore: seen from the sky,
the lake is the grey and white sky. Today
I am raking the gravel of my driveway, trapped,
as Picasso was trapped. The stone
slips through the teeth of the rake
with a low sound, like a hammer
striking a small clay bell. The lake burns a hundred metres away,
through the lilies of the valley and the cloud anemones,
casting me, and my rake,
against the trees on the far shore,
as light. This is a particularly human problem.

That Picasso has come back into the stillness of a pebble
is, however, also a particularly
human problem, and that is why I am raking the gravel today,
in the dimensionless air after grey rain,
the clouds towering above the hills
as the black terns lift mosquitoes off the face of the lake
and swallow them. They taste like grass. A skiff
of wind spills in a slow, silver arc across the water
and the tiny, two-inch fish — the spring's spawn —
break the surface with their lips,
like stones, skipping,
then sink back into the reflected trees.

Drawing Hands

for Robin Skelton

I wanted to draw hands that touch fire.
All I had before me were Michelangelo's
yellowed studies and my short, thick hands,
and shavings and rubber wisps. I thought of your hands,
rich with the watery stones of the earth,
carrying the weight of history through the years
as they shimmer and clang with their moon-beaten power.
Like the students, whose hands are mutilated,
misshaped, warped, with spindly,
bent fingers or grotesque swollen thumbs,
my hands lay recognizable
only by the intent. Yours are famous. People
come now not to hear your poetry
but to see the ancient, haunting power of a hand
that swept the granary floor clear of stars
and began to thresh the dark into skeins of grass.
I walked out tonight with my five-month-old daughter
along the diked and flood-green river
under a blue heron moon. The leaves
flashed huge and silent —
our thoughts arranged in song: flaring,
footsteps in the dance,
the wild unbeaten light. You sit
awake tonight, your fingers
over the pages scattered out before you,
listening too through your hands.
The silence opens into time.
The crystals form around the core of fire.
The hands reach out and touch and bless.

Birdsong

Now that the winter everyone said I would be unable to bear
is past and the suckers are spawning
in the clear water between the ice and the sedges,
every day one of the days I passed through in '82,
looking North for apple land,
with the green miles slipping past, the black trees,
comes in struggling, dust in its throat, coughing,
and that journey into the earth
for the mystical valley of pines and thin snow,
sheltered from the white owls of northern cold
by the sea blowing up the Skeena,
is all my journeys — although all we found
in Cedarvale was one old farm
with sour, worm-choked apples
in a cardboard box on the windowsill,
and the light as if it were squeezed from grass.

Today I feed the robins the last of my winter apples
and walk down to the shore
among the saskatoons and kinnikinic,
but instead of my high plateau lake
the small, white, wooden church at Hazelton,
just up the hill from the Skeena,
rides the light like foam — flanked by wrecked cars and
                              powerlines,
gravel, overgrown grass crushed down by snow,
and weeds. The Coast Mountains thunder high with snow
behind it.

Standing among the shore willows and dwarf brown birches
I am at a loss, facing this day driven from the land,
that has no other place to go
in the blue world. Whistling swans
strut across the white spring ice —
breath of the moon. Blackbirds
flare up over the reeds and settle down
on the mud-flats, flashing, red and black. I step
over the marshy spring grass —
into the dust and ghosts. The floorboards
echo. I sit near the front, to hear,
and slowly, as I grow still there,
I make out the guttural voices of the dead —
the roar of trucks on the Yellowhead
between Rupert and Prince George
spilling in through the window like glass
and across the floor as a square of light,

but the air is sparkling and I lose the sound
in the dancing dust. I stand from the pew,
for the birds are singing all around me:
bulrush tongues,
dragonfly voices squeezed into bone:
deafening.

The Kingfisher

Charles Hill-Tout, 1858–1944

At the mouth of Penticton Creek
there is one black power wire
where the creek spills from the Penticton Industrial Area
and the suburbs flanking it
into the slow, dredged, diked channel
of the Okanagan River. I drive past once a week,
bringing my daughter home from dance class.
As I swing into the bypass traffic
the kingfisher is always there, with his blue crown,
half an hour before dusk, fishing,
in the roar of traffic. He stares
over the sawmill on the Indian Reserve —
whole forests rotting, huge grey piles of wood
logged off solely to be transformed into that picture of power
and uselessness, a pure distillation of industrial purpose.
The kingfisher stares beyond that, to the purple hills,
all the trees raking up, black and jagged,
burnt by a tourist's cigarette.

I trespass in memory. My heart pounds.
The deep crystal water of Keremeos Creek flows past me, living.
All spring and summer a mountain of cull potatoes
sprouted and fermented and shrivelled
in a clattering cloud of grasshoppers
just past the potato sorting machine — a huge
post-industrial sculpture of green and rusting
sheet metal and chain-belts. Beyond that cloud,
through tangles of nightshade and dogwood,
the overgrown lilac and lily gardens of the Richter Ranch —
a collapsed latticework gazebo and sprawling yellow roses

climbing up the trunks of alders and Rocky Mountain maples —
the kingfisher would sit on a lightning-snapped
cottonwood on the edge of the island, diving
in front of my line to snatch an electric, silver trout
from the pool before me, 10,000 volts,
with his headdress, and the light of the sky caught in his
                                        feathers;
in the cool colours of memory, the threads of sunlight
in water now burnt dry by fast run-off, the whole stream bed
dredged by the ranchers of Olalla, for flood control.

He cannot be seen by anyone who has not already seen.
I have walked out with Charles Hill-Tout
as he tried to divine for water
at the Indian Reserve on the bunchgrass hills
skirting Penticton. Hill-Tout moved slowly westward, walking up
through prickly pear and wild onions,
the iridescent green beetles, the loose gravel
of the old creekbed, the anemones and sage,
with a forked stick pointed at the grass
and the wind tearing at his cloak. The church was still new,
its white paint burning. I stood in the doorway
with the blue sun flaming behind me,
as Hill-Tout tried to write down a few words of the old language;
and listened, there, silent,
and a few children around me.
The sun burnt through the door,
a grouse bursting out of a sagebrush
just in front of my feet, tearing off in a low,
veering flight, whimpering and screeching,
the creaking strain on each feather heard,
held on the air — a violin with strings of grass,
a cricket dreaming in its sleep, what a cricket hears
as it rasps itself to sleep
in a crack in a wall, in the growing cold;
and I held silent, though it stung.

The Trickster Years

—

TAKING THE BREATH AWAY (1987–1997)

THE BLUE MOUTH OF MORNING (1994–1998)

The City without Angels

Freiburg im Breisgau

Long ago the angels lived in doorways.
Whenever people went in and out,
the angels had to step into the streets.
If it had snowed they were terribly cold:
all they had for shoes were sandals
woven out of reeds.

In that old city people had built shelter for themselves
and for their livestock:
they'd built nothing for the holy birds.
Whenever it rained and the wind blew out of the west,
the angels sought refuge in the cathedral,

but the cathedral was built of stone: high, dark,
and cold. It held only a few low wooden pews,
without pillows, without blankets.
The angels would lay themselves out there head to head
and stare the whole night
thoughtfully at the dark stone sky.

On Sundays it was even worse: the people streamed out of the
                                        narrow alleys
into the cathedral. There was no room left for the angels:
they had to stand outside in the square — in the hot sunlight,
                                        in the snow,
and in the black rain of the world.

In the nave the choir sang as beautifully as the boys
who sat on the knees of God and ate grapes out of his hands,
but in the square the angels watched the monsters
on the peak of the roof, listened to the hymns, and did not
sing a note, and said no word. They simply
waited until the people were finished.
They had blue faces. They were half frozen.
You see them now and think they are made out of stone.
They stand in gaps in the wall
and on the roof: solid, yet they are not made out of stone.
They are made out of the song of the choir
and the red mouths of women.

They are waiting for us.
They know very well that they must wait
a long, long time. They have prepared themselves
for that. They have transformed themselves from ambassadors
into Waiting itself, while a black rain falls
in the night of the cities
and the doors in the empty gaps of the wall
are newly painted and tightly closed.

The City of Witches

Freiburg im Breisgau

In the city of witches the starlight
catches in the narrow canals
that flow out of the forest into the lake;
if the tails of two cows become tangled,
the most pious young women give one
woman up to the men, who burn her
under the walls at noon;
in the hot sun the smoke pours up blackly,
and smoky flashes of fire and the woman's screams
float up over the steep roofs
into the white mouth of the sun.
Over the city of witches the sun is huge
and fills most of the sky.
After the burning, the women walk home
through the streets: at first a long column,
then breaking off house by house,
until each woman steps in alone
through her black door.

Late in the afternoon the sun burns
in the narrow channels of water
that flow through the city
from the forest into the reeds
twice the height of a man,
and burns on the face of the water.
The women have clay jugs
which they dip into the streams
of golden fire. When they lift the jugs
the water is black: terrified,
and careful not to spill a drop,

they hurry back into their houses
without saying a word.

When the men built the cathedral
for their women, they threw the scrap stone
into the lake, cartload after cartload,
which they hauled down with heavy brown horses
breathing clouds in the cool morning.
The stone slipped into the water
without disturbing the surface
or raising the level of the water,
and the men know: the lake
is bottomless. They are quick with their work
and are careful not to slip in.
When one of them accidentally falls into the water
they pull him out immediately, by the hair if they have to,
for the men in the city of witches
do not know how to swim.

A Private Screening

The young man
with the earring
and the red hair

who travelled from England
to his mother's
magic house
under the oaks
in Victoria

to show his father
a film from Ireland
of Ben Bulben
and the blue streams
in which William Butler
Yeats fished

for salmon
and of the black
stone and ivy tower that
was his home

after he plotted revolution
with a green-eyed
red-haired woman
in a park
full of water lilies
and white swans

is dead too young
with only his mother
and his lover to hold
him and help him go
where we all
must soon

It is fitting
that the movie
ended with a walk
into a country
churchyard
with low walls of stone
set not to keep
anything or anyone
in or out
but to define simply
a space
to hold the charm
Cast a cold eye
On life on death.
Horseman, pass by!
then the clear wind
over the brown
winter heather
and the clouds
streaming shredding
building in the sky

The sound
of the borrowed projector
did not matter
the chatter of conversation
with all the small
foot-high
goddesses on the mantel
behind the white and silver
screen

added only a richness
to the film
the accent of whose narrator
I could scarcely understand
but which held the youth
of the young man's father
when he travelled to Ireland
to drink porter and to beg
the dialect
from door to door
and so learn his craft
as a poet
in ancient
Ireland

It was the only time
I ever met the young
man with the single earring
and the flaming
red hair
although I love his mother
and his white-bearded
father well have eaten blood
sausage in the green
walled kitchen
have pruned
the apricot tree
growing over the glass
of the solarium
in the back of his mother's magic
and unpainted house
and feel blessed
to have been invited there
to share that
moment
together in Victoria
by the sea

The oaks flare out
over the roof of the house
like a crown
and move all night
and are never still
they are very strong

Beneath them
and in their shade
the old King apples bloom
and swell
and grow on black
and purple limbs
covered with lichen
and pale green moss

while beside them
the house trembles
and shifts
and sighs

for the man and woman
who live within her
to whom she is home
and shelter

as are the trees
as is the light
as is the air

The Fish

lie on the wall-to-wall carpet
while I listen to Bach.
They are small and yellow.
Trout swim slowly through the sunbeams
in the firs. The tuna are shadows.
They breathe our death in and our lives out.

Late at night I lie down in bed.
Instead of my wife, I find a salmon beside me.
She lays her head on the pillow and sorrowfully
watches me with the eyes of the sea.

In the spring, blue fish
swim in the face of the moon.
When the clouds drive in tatters,
the fish swim out into the purple sea.
They fall to the earth as rain.
They stream over my face.
I catch them with my hands.

They flow off the roof through the down-pipe
and into the flower beds,

with the voices of birds,
that live under the earth
and have been calling us quietly

since the beginning of time.

Home on the Range

In June Mozart moves out to the range
and rides the bulls as they slip, black,
through white-trunked aspens. As he rides,
he sings arias under his breath,
old Hank Williams songs from the radio,
and something new, a kind of music
that sounds like starlight blowing through trees
and coyotes yipping from stone-dry arroyos.

In the height of summer he brings the bulls down
from the rangeland to the city. In a dusty field
between the railroad and lumber yards,
cowboys ride his bulls for money and fame.

Mozart dresses as a clown.
When a cowboy is thrown,
Mozart steps in the bull's path
and sings arias from *Don Giovanni*
and the *Barber of Seville.*
While the cowboy scrambles away, the bull
nuzzles Mozart's hand for a cube of sugar.

Mozart has trained the cows as well;
when he rides on the shoulders of the lead bull,
back up the silver rivers and red-stone washes
into the rangeland, the cows stand with their calves
among the trees, singing in chorus.

As the stars flow and swirl
in vast currents overhead, the gold
gradually settles out
in the deeper pools, until slowly,
over the shoulder of the land,
it is day, and the clouds tower over the forests
all the way to the sea.

Paradise Found

Back in the '50s Shakespeare used to run a skidder
out of Anaheim Lake,
but now he's opened a lawnmower repair shop
amidst the old singlewides and rusty Chevrolets of Lac La
                                                    Hache,
and charges by the hour. The walls of his shop
are plastered with sonnets, printed in the pale colours
of the '40s, the paper yellowed with the years.
The floor is dirt packed hard as cement,
littered with old greasy gears,
piston heads, and shining carburetor needles.
Shakespeare is in the back by the grinder,
a blue welder's cap covering his skinny, bald head,
a spray of sparks shooting around him
while he grinds the slag off a half-molten piston
to the tune of the low-pitched roar
that sinks off the stone.

Down the highway from Shakespeare's Lawnmower Repair
John Milton, whose eyesight has been restored
by swimming through the river of silence,
has settled his daughters in a fly-tying shop.
There is nothing fancy here, and nothing is arranged for
                                                    tourists,
but John has been fishing in Lac La Hache and Rail Lake
and the glacial and horsefly country of the Chilcotin
for sixty years and has learned a thing or two
in that time.

Most any day you will find him in an old Coors Lite t-shirt,
a pot-belly hanging over his jeans,
peering over the tops of his bifocals
at delicate watercolours of chironomids and mayflies

that look like fairies, that look able to grace us
with a love more intense than cut flowers,
and which he painstakingly copies with deerhide, coloured
                                                    thread
and wood-duck feathers.

If you want to find his daughters
you will have to canoe onto the lake,
for they spend their days there,
clear-skinned, scooping the latest hatch off the water,
where wings gleam white
against the deep without light,
thoughts floating on the first age of the world;
and painting them on heavy rag paper
with handmade sow's bristle brushes.

This is their share of the work now,
and after his passage through blindness
John is glad of it.

On Mondays John hangs the closed sign in the front window
and goes onto the lake with his neighbour.
In the middle of the lake, Shakespeare cuts the old Evinrude
and they drift with the slow current;
he drops a line with lead weights and a lurid
pink and green plug over the stern
and is content to lie back
watching the pattern of the clouds
drift across the gentian sky, but Milton is not.
He stands in the prow
and with deft flicks of his wrist
casts a fly far out onto the still black
ahead of them, into absolute emptiness,
into the pure definition of water,
and with trembling fingers and a pounding heart
waits for a fish to rise and strike hard.

The Scent of the Earth

Coyote has answered one of those real estate ads
for a lakeshore farm in the high country
with a view off the edge of the plateau
to the mountains
cloaked in blue shadow and white glaciers,
against whose slopes clouds form
like breath on a winter morning —

and he is a farmer now
according to the custom
of the land. Today he has hooked up the tractor
to an old two-bottom plough. As the diesel
exhaust spills over his face
and leaves fall, a yellow avalanche
as thick as February snow,
he ploughs his fields
into the black waves of the sea.

In the cool of dusk, when the air is pale lavender,
he cuts the throttle and walks
across the furrows in sudden, hammering silence,
his hands smelling of his leather gloves,
until he sees the first star
rise above the glacier.

As the frost settles out of the quartz air,
he sits on the bare, black soil,
waiting for the first fish to rise
from the glacial stones.

By midnight, all the old roofs of the farm,
the white poplars,
the distant peaks, and the faces of the furrows
glow with the silver light of fish,
and Coyote rises and calls. And the fish come

slowly, impossibly, out of the land,
bucking, heaving,
and breaking free,
swimming down the cut sods,
out through the neighbouring meadows
of wheatgrass and sedges,
and into the sky.

It is a form of farming
which brings no monetary return
and produces no produce for sale
or even for consumption,
and although Coyote had to mortgage himself for years
down in the valleys
to purchase the farm, he does not allow himself to think
that he owns this land: he is simply glad
to be able to return it to the sky
and to sit all night in the scent of the earth.

Plato's Penance

Plato has given up on the just order
of life among men;
with breath rich from Player's tobacco
and fingers orange from hand-rolled cigarettes,
he runs a timber-cruising company
out of Williams Lake.

His office is the front room
of a fifty-year-old clapboard house,
in the fly-ash from the mill
and the hammering of the night trains.

In the blue-and-white television flicker
he sits on his Naugahyde couch,
his papers spread around him,
charting the timber of cut-blocks
in the sacred land spoken
at the beginning of the world.

He will admit readily
he once tried to fashion a world based on exclusion
and the manipulation of thought
through embodiments of rhetoric
in the forms of the world.

He will apologize: If you visit,
he will sweep aside the styrofoam cups,
turn down the volume,
and out of bleary eyes
as grey as the distant sea
tell how in the Chilcotin
he almost lost his head to a trip wire
laid to catch wild horses

that eat grass which otherwise could be grazed
by cattle.

He was riding skidoo,
checking out the parameters of a stand —
lodgepole pine mostly,
a few firs and aspens by the lakes —
when he went down.

The horses are quartered with chainsaws,
hauled to town in pickups,
and sold as pet food. As Plato speaks,
you see in his eyes the mares
running wild across the eastern slopes,
their copper manes flowing.
Very pointedly Plato returns to his calculations —
the number of cubic feet per hectare.
In his eyes the green crowns of the trees
surge in a deep wind off the sea.

Sometimes Plato goes for breakfast at the all-night hotel.
He stays all morning smoking in the café
with a view of his old legacy,
the BC Rail switching yard,
full of coal cars and lumber cars heading south.
Because he can make no sense of his shame,
when the bar opens at noon
he goes in and watches women
strip down to their certainty.

He once wrote of cicadas,
women singing from hot stones,
memory — stripped from us —
given to the mute things of this earth.
At night he returns home
to work, his mind drenched with horses.

Return to Open Water

Charles Lillard, 1944–1997

The whales call from the traffic
and Red comes to ride them
with a halter made of an old winch cable
He speaks to them in Chinook
In his pocket he carries a handful of trade beads
which he has promised to the Beaufort Sea

As the whales buck along Douglas Street
Red stands on the back of the lead whale
the cable cinched tightly around his left wrist
his right hand held out for balance
clutching a weatherbeaten hat like a young kid
at Anaheim Lake in July
When the traffic stalls at the Fort Street light
the exhaust pours over him like morning fog
over the herring beds
and he steadies his foothold
and holds on

As the whales pass through the downtown core
bucking and swaying
the cod begin to rise out of the alleys and loading zones
the herring descend in great shoals from the clouds
and the salmon slip out of the plate glass
They all flow down through the apartments of James Bay
the daffodils and gorse
picking up cod and mackerel bream and surf perch
then stream into the Strait of Juan de Fuca
and west through the brass gates Bawlf says Drake saw there
marking the end of the world and the entrance of Eldorado

Red is not going to Eldorado
Red is going to sea

—

In Eldorado
we dress in gold
We deck our hair in feathers
dipped in pollen
We rub clay on our cheeks
Day and night the foundries
spark with molten gold
and the hammering of the goldsmiths
pours down every street
Books are brought in from the forest
where they have changed themselves
into birds
to hide from the fires
at the end of the world
And our goldsmiths
hammer them out flat
into the rain
into the scales of salmon
the eyes of halibut
staring out of the floor
of the sea

Red has them in his pocket
loose change for his voyage

We stand on shore
our golden clothes sparkle
in the sun
our turquoise rings
glow on our fingers

like eyes turned blind
eyes that can only
see the earth

—

A man stands in my doorway.
His body is fire.

I dress him in wind. He becomes the rain.

I dress him in rain. He becomes the sun.

I dress him in sun. He becomes the grass.

I dress him in grass. He becomes the wind.

Blowing away all memory.

Blowing away all rain,
all sun, all grass.

Blowing away.

No man stands
in my doorway.

I do not wake.
I have become the sea.

The Renaissance Confessional Boxes

When I was still a small child, I had no skin at all;
every movement of the wind flowed directly into my blood.
In Autumn, when fish threw themselves
out of the white lakes into the air, I shivered with cold,
for carried by the current of the wind, the stars
had settled in my bones. My fingers glowed
with the tongues of birds. The doctors
had no answers. They tried to sew me a skin: leaves, plastic,
paper, cotton, leather and parachute nylon would not stick
and fell to the ground. After that, the doctors
went back to their field hospitals with trembling fingers,
and left me to find my own cure.

Underneath an apple tree I found an old book of poetry
and discovered a skin in there, while blue birds
flew through the leaves. This skin was strong
and thin, supple and full of colours, was sewn out of frogs
and flies, clouds and the motion of wind over the water
of a glacial lake. It fitted me perfectly.
For many years now I have worn this skin with pride —
whether I have stood in a grey city or on a mountain —
and everyone has noticed that a wind stood before them,
cool and damp. Now I look at old pictures in my album
and notice, shaken, that one is of a stranger, smiling,
another is of the moon, in another yellow leaves
lie on wet black soil under poplars while the sun
turns into a snow cloud — in yet another
there is snow, nothing more.

The sun lies on the bottom of the sea,
drinks water, shapes it into eggs of light,
and buries them in gravel.

The wind is a tree.

Now I am trying to take off this skin, but there are no buttons,
and it does not tear. Without pride I have to say
that I am my skin that I found in an old book of poetry; that
                                   when I page
through the album now, in the purple- and blue-shadowed snow,
I find nothing except the moon, the sun, and the world
that I must slowly, word by word, build out of the invisible,

so that there are still pictures.

The City is Famous for Libraries and Houses of Music

In the library of the musicians
there are no books,
no recordings, and no instruments,
yet of all the libraries
it is the most visited. In the long aisles
are stacked rain, stones, rivers, birds
balancing on black, fog-drenched twigs.

Everyone who enters
finds his or her self
standing stock-still
in a far aisle
as the sun breaks through mist.

Throughout the library
musicians step forward
slowly,
so as not to frighten their bodies,
touching them at first gently
on the shoulders. When their bodies turn
and recognize their place,
the musicians draw them close
and cradle them.
in arms
that have held the snow
and have not held snow.

Everyone who enters the library enters alone.

No one leaves.

The Message

From the city
men lead camels
into the shifting sand.

They are watched for hours
from the highest towers

by men in red robes,
until they vanish, tiny,
into the mirroring wall of heat —

then the watchers cry out
with a long, drawn-out wail of joy
sung deep in the throat.

The travellers have hawks on their wrists
and messages in their pockets.
They are on their way
to the king.

The message they bring
is a tiny silver box
that when opened in daylight,
as the sand whips in
off the streets,
contains the sun, and when shut
contains instantaneously
its absence,
which was there before it.

It is the simplest thing in the world,
but also the most inscrutable.

The men let the hawks go free;
the hawks return with empty claws;

while the king is unaware
that a message is on its way
from the world.

The Dramatic Years

—

FREE WILL (2002–2004)

Telling the Truth

When someone asks you for the truth,
for God's sake, lie. Give them what they want.

And if they ask again, lie a second time,
a third, a fourth, until you're hoarse;

sign every paper they slide across to you,
their finger on the line, where they ask you

for your house, your car, your stocks;
pay the interest on your debt, accept the truth,

stand before the camera and tell them how it was,
how it's all true — you blew up that bridge,

stole those plans, took your boss's wife
to Palm Beach; for you have been to Hell

and back these last few weeks, and deserve
no less than an end to lies, fine print,

and sound bites, not to mention sleep,
what with all you've had to swallow

just to stand here in my place and defend
those actions you know nothing of,

denied a chance to say what you do know,
while I stand in for you, with my briefcase

and my files, whispering in your ear, that what
you say in this court matters not,

that you know yourself at last (I squeeze
your arm), that truth is a lie.

from The Uncollected Sonnets of Mr. W.S., Translated from the English

Sonnet 155: The Heist

I've got to hand it to you, the way you pulled it off:
despite all the guards, the cameras, the infrared,

you stole my heart, that sparkled like cut glass.
Now security has brought in tracking dogs,

dusted for fingerprints, and put word out
on the street to find the thief. Like the rest, I say

I don't know who did this deed — except I lie.
The gallery is empty, the lights turned up;

men with coveralls search with microscopes;
I should lock myself in Nice and weep,

but I just can't. Right now my heart is racing
through Beirut. We came in at night — a fishing boat.

The salt was sharp. The dark swells
were a shock. I shuddered in delight. Ah,

there's the shop, a door in back, a gentle knock,
three times like a bird cracking a nut, and we're

inside. I can barely stand it, the way we walk — I say we,
but I am carried, I know, and the man in black

is walking, with strong footsteps on the carpet —
towards soft words, cups of tea, bright light. Ah,

I am laid out on a velvet pillow, and you
pick me up at last and hold me up,

beloved. Your heart is stolen too,
you thief, don't tell me it isn't.

Sonnet 157: In the Lineup

I am in the lineup with other thieves
and dealers from the street,

in the glare of light. You stand
behind the mirror with a Styrofoam cup

of coffee and the pigs, who grunt at us
through the mic, *Turn to the left.*

(It's like a line dance in a country hall.
I throw back my head and sashay up.)

and *Have the short one step forward
and blow a kiss.* I'm caught! I sweat

and step out of the line, knowing you undress me
right there, in front of the cops, the crooks,

the guards. They probably have the whole thing
spooled on tape. When you leave, they'll give

you a copy of the cassette, which you
can play at home whenever you want

to watch me twist, but what I want
to know is when you caught that kiss

on your cruel cheek, did you want to rush down
swept by laughter or did you think instead,

Tie him up!, because I can't stand here
much longer without a charge in court,

and if I'm going to plead guilty I need to know what
sentence you will give, or do I get house arrest?

Without a Clue

I started without a clue of who killed the guest
in the Highland castle by the loch,

with the salmon rising under the ice of the burn
that sang all summer over rills,

the foxes running through the snow
and heather burning on the fire.

It is a land of ghosts, of men betrayed,
a people sold to foreign power,

water steeped in peat and set aside
in burnt oak for all the years

of a woman's beauty,
the lonely walks across the moor,

the bracing wind, and women,
who don't pray to gods or God, and men

who say they do, but pray
to themselves instead,

expecting an answer when they kneel
before an altar of devotion,

while women wait — not theirs in the least —
between ironed sheets,

too cold to sleep. My experience so far
in this distant place as near as kin

is none will come.
The place drives men apart.

The women talk of lives past
and lives to come as if they're past

and only speech is left before a fire.
Men drink the smoke.

The obsequious butler, the retired India man
who knows enough of slaughter,

the starlet from the South, who pretends
to know the nothing the wisest know

is the nothing that will slay them in the end,
and all the other guests, the poet,

who rhymes the heather with the weather,
(he drinks too much champagne

and cries for attention),
the medium (the accent's fake),

the prime minister (retired),
the mayor from the village,

who talks too loud, the prince
(a case study for any kid who's reading Freud),

all know that one of them is marked for death,
that their presence is a crime they will commit

and so must answer to, no matter how they struggle
to turn it to laughter as candles dance

above a table set with silver
and crystal goblets and claret.

The pheasant steams, the windows set with lead,
such tiny panes, each one leaking wind.

The fox is wild. The night is his.
All know it, and laugh to forget.

The stars that rise blue above the snow
and fall through fog are the cold men know

in those dark halls, but not the cold
that drives the fox, and not the cold of God.

That is the cold we come to in the end.
We're not there yet, but we are close.

It is the women, dressed in red,
who throw the heather on and smell it burn

even in their sleep, if they can sleep
with no warmth but their own

between the sheets and dream
the dream that is all that is.

Iago's Version

Backstage, the birds were everywhere — nuthatches and lyre
                                                    birds,
eagles and grosbeaks. Starlings fluttered in Romeo's face,
twittering like children in the Gaza Strip.
Romeo couldn't slay Tybalt — he couldn't see him.
Nightingales hung onto the rose arbour and trilled like violins.
When Juliet cried, *A rose by any other name*
would smell as sweet, Romeo heard the birds
and saw the moon with its hollow corpse's face, puckering.

Othello rolled over — on his pillow there was a shrike
that had flown from the Euphrates with a ball of mud.
You couldn't hold down a conversation.
It was fine for an evening,
but it went on for years.

After a decade, none of us thought anymore.
Actors swung around lamp posts.
They sang "Singing in the Rain"
in a language made of grunts and squeaks.
They picked lice. They made love in public.
They carried their children on their backs.
They slept on their roofs under the stars
while the monkeys moved among them
with bullwhips and serums,
writing everything down meticulously,
asdrilk&8()(* with ashtray, Bonsai with %%^/1jd,
but no-one could read it, except God,
and for him it was the book of the world.
He lived within it. He wanted a door;
yet wherever he looked out through long rooms,
the ceiling fans framed against
the black grates of the balconies,
there was an ostrich or a heron or a kite.

There were so many parrots, he couldn't see past them:
he had a thousand doors; there was no way out
that was not blocked by peahens and bitterns,
which had become a sentence
in a syntax that would not end.

For every improvised scene the librarians cut
from the chimpanzees' manuscripts —
the scene of Rosalind reading *Chatelaine*
while having her nails done, the scene of Shylock
eating kosher dills in a Montreal deli —
our world backstage became more empty,
more like a wind blowing from the farthest stars
across the keys of Bach's harpsichord,
chilling his fingers; less like a world at all.

The scene of Oberon fitting his rainbow codpiece, cut,
the scene of Falstaff planting tobacco in Virginia, cut —
until there was just one last scrap of a scene
in the bottom of the in-tray. The librarians lifted it out,
turned it over, read it backwards, forwards,
the light of trees washing over their faces,
branches swaying in wind five minutes after rain,
read it until there was nothing left of it,
until the letters were all invisible,
having passed from this world into the mind.

What had been a play lay before them in ruins.
They poked at it with a pen —
the image of monkeys laughing on one scrap of paper.
When they looked at it directly, there was nothing.
They had to catch it out of the corner of an eye.

So is it possible to see the world outside of reason,
the light playing on the edge of a room,
rain passing in chainlink sheets
across the face of a spring mountain,
the scent of pine needles, and actors looking up
to see clouds, forming in living air,
dissipate in the wind,
and reading themselves there.

Oh What Fools These Mortals Be

Phoenix Summer Theatre, 1975

Today Robin Goodfellow is a Cox's orange pippin,
nestled among leaves.

The sun glints off a sheen of wax.
The scent of bees wafts from heavy grass.

Robin is waiting, waiting, waiting.
He swells around the sweet juice

in the languages of men — in this moment
together we are the language of birds,

and you who I am are surrounded by students
on a wooden stage; they are dressed in gauze;

they speak their lines so seriously
it's as if they had become books.

All the time Robin hangs from the lights,
sometimes by the crook of a single toe,

and whispers and buzzes and crackles and laughs —
bright fire on a summer night.

Robin can take on all the parts:
the heartbroken men from the boarding house,

Hermia who puts it out every night in the dorm,
her skin like butter melting in the mouth.

Smoochie, smoochie, mouths Robin,
almost losing his balance.

Shhhhh! softer on that footfall.
You're supposed to sound like a faery,

a garland around a girl's throat,
green stem to white blossom.

Look! Here comes Theseus,
king of the ape men,

dressed in his tights and his cape,
with his voice dropped down low

like the bottom of the sea,
leading a bull by the nose

through the circles of the mind,
la de da. God, pretty Lysander,

look at him! He's hung like a horse. Jesus!
Instead of him, the audience sees some farm kid

dressed in tights
and makeup like splintered glass —

reds and yellows and greens across his face,
his hair a bird's nest in an apricot tree

in late October, when the storms come
and the heart shivers

and crawls down into the feet
and will not budge.

Good god, yells Robin,
swinging down from the light bar

and landing on the stage with a thump
as the kid sweeps the stage clear

and the lovers have found each other
and embrace. Actually, if you see it from the back,

Demetrius is groping Helena
and she is sliding into the crook of his arm,

her breasts warm, her thighs
like the first page of *War and Peace*.

Ah, it really is a world of such promise,
winks Robin, copping a feel, then turning.

Can that actually be me? A soft whisper.
Running his green fingers over the boy's soft cheeks.

And just for a second
Robin has a shotglass of pity

and speaks out of the boy's voice,
If we have offended,

then breaks into laughter,
and skips off,

leaving the boy on the stage,
confused and alone with a set piece.

"Give me your hands
and all is mended."

God what is that supposed to mean?
But the crowd with their la de da claps,

and the men from the rooming house
wave from the front row,

with their grey faces
and the treacle on their teeth.

The tree goes out. In the darkness a bird trills.
The orchard is all around,

empty; the mountains rise up,
as if you released a spring

in the back of a picture frame
made of pipe smoke,

in which black and white people
stare out quizzically. Years later,

the dark voice of Oberon calls out to the boy,
Theseus dressed in drag,

and sometimes in the night,
when the world is still

and all the voices that make up memory
are off to the thickets of the forest,

the boy hears a small voice cry out
from the gold leaf pressed into the frame,

Captain of our fairy band!
Helena is here at hand.

And the youth mistook by me,
pleading for a lover's fee.

The light over the trees
that stretch around the you I am

sparkles like waves on the water,
until Robin comes over

and closes your eyelids with his finger,
and the last you see is the darkness,

and the last you taste is an apple
warm in the sun.

Gertrude's Version

Hamlet Redux

Gertrude is in the dairy room,
arranging flowers
and fruit
around her husband's body,
with cold water
running down the walls
and the smell of dark.

Beside her stands
a servant girl
from the village,
the blacksmith's daughter,
in her first blush,
her hair like rain —
hired by the king
with a nod
from his coach.

The girl is trembling
as Gertrude sticks
a newton pippin
in her husband's mouth
and slips a sprig
of parsley
into the grey hairs
around his prick. The apple
is warmer than the man,
she notes, and pauses.
There is the sound of breaking
chairs

coming from the main hall
and glasses
smashed into a grate.

The girl holds a candle.
She is only a face
rising above the light,
bleeding into darkness
at the edges
and reforming.

Gertrude remembers little
of her life
before she stepped
into this room —
how Raleigh came one afternoon
to the theatre
dressed as the sun,
and the Queen with him,
dressed as a spider
that had taken on the mask
of the queen of the fairies,
who takes lovers
as she will.

For a moment you could not tell
who was on stage and who
was the audience. When Gertrude saw
gold cloth sewn through Raleigh's jerkin,
she forgot her lines blankly.
Who knows what she said
in those few minutes
when she passed
from the South Bank of London
into Denmark and damnation.

The crowd roared.
She thought she heard fighting.
She was sure the Queen
came on stage
and switched places with her,
that Raleigh became king.

She no longer believes
anything can be set right.
She remembers city streets,
traffic, the long
yellow lawns of Hyde Park
rising into smoky air,
her childhood in the Blitz,
the empty blocks, smashed crockery,
crowds in Piccadilly Circus,
and the long years of absence and rain
when the greasepaint kept her sane.

That is all gone.
She is hiding in the cellar
with the corpse of a king
who stands on the top battlement
and crows at the rising of the sun
in a stain of blood
out of the sea.

The theatre has become a skull,
a toothless mouth, blind eyes staring
where there was a mind,
wind above a high path
over breaking waves,
and no expectation.
She hears laughter, the slippery sounds
of a man and woman fucking,
and the woman cries out —
she screams as she comes;
a shudder runs through cloven air.

In the silence that follows,
the world vanishes.
There is no servant girl,
no dead husband,
no castle. There is no candle.
The stars whirl around Gertrude.
A hunting bird screams at great height.
When the king steps up behind her,
as big as the sky,
to slip his tongue into her ear,
slipping his hands over her breasts,

she looks straight ahead,
where the sea breaks
against the castle walls,
afraid to turn.
If she looks into his eyes,
it will all become real:
she will forget even London,
she will forget she was a girl
who took to theatre
for poetry and the beauty,
the strength that came
from being the voice
of a poem itself
and the world.

And so the play will not pass its time.
The girl she was speaks, out of her fear,
of herbs and flowers
and healing, into the dark
where the audience once sat,

and hears out there a wild voice
slip down from tier to tier,
leap into the pit
and step across it slowly,
listening

greedily
for what she will do
now

that she is on her own.

Desdemona's Wedding

Desdemona dresses in her grave clothes
for her wedding to the Moor, dyes her hair pink
and wears a pin in her tit, slips
out of bed at night, sports studded collars
and crawls on her knees through stone streets
that night she married Othello
and the sea fell to the stars.
Venice drew a cape around itself
and men drank it like wine
as the tide suckled their houses.

And even that happened too slowly.
Between jealous rage and a feather pillow
over lips that sought to speak a cry
of reason or a word of love,
whole centuries passed,
navies sailed out and sank in smoke,
armies bled in muddy streets,
men were dispatched like pigs,
Mozart composed his symphonies,
Beethoven went deaf, Schumann mad,

so don't say that thing
about Desdemona, that gossip about the Moor,
the right of conquest,
the soldier's lance, and don't ever
say the expected thing, that love is madness,
that the only madness is in the mind.
To have a mind is madness.
Pray you can hold out five minutes
between your wedding and *your* death.

Grief

It is the way we make what is be what we are,
however briefly, however we may aspire

to more than the sobs that shake us loose
of what we were and what we will become,

to hold us here just a little longer,
where we don't understand what brought us

to this stasis and this end, how the tumor started,
spread, the black hours beside the bed,

the meters, tubes, the nurse who comes
with catheters, morphine, a low voice, rubber shoes,

day and night, calls us gently by the name she knows us
by, until she comes one night before the dawn,

pulls the plug, brushes down the lids,
while we sit among the flowers we have brought

and all the symbols of a life now passed
we cannot find our way to down any hall.

No door leads out. The doctors nod.
We don't wander out but in.

It is our grief we become at last,
and all who see us in the next weeks —

our eyes bloodshot, living on pills,
giving a speech to friends in a windy field

because she would enter no church
where the voice was caged, sprinkling ashes

to be caught and blown away into the unsayable,
signing papers, reading wills,

packing her clothing in a box
and lying in the empty bed that was a field

of roses and now is cold as snow —
do not see the lives we were,

the death we have become, but the door
that swings between them both and lets us in

to let us out. We are wandering now, out in the snow,
while the world sleeps, free of pain,

and dreams at last the dream of knowledge
we can only grieve.

The Lyrical Years
—

NEW POEMS (2003–2007)

In a Forest House

In my house I hear a woman's footsteps
step across the waves of wheat
that break against her clapboard house
east of the high coolies of hawks and sun
in Washington and feel waves shudder
as they strike the sand of Carolina beaches.
A lizard that skitters across a rock in Tijuana
whispers in my house, as if a woman
were slipping across the carpet to draw back blinds
to let the sun across a bed, dappled with shade.

I live in a forest house. A house by the sea
listens to eternity, the first word of God,
the calls of whales, echoing between Wrangell
and Tiero del Fuego, the flash of salmon, the sun
cascading through cathedrals of kelp,
and when waves break at Tofino
feels the waves crash from Hokkaido to Santiago
and not the beach a few steps down from a door
stained with salt and painted green.

A forest house has roots and does not ride the swells.
It is not a house in which to set to sea,
the hold packed with biscuits and beans,
blue willow china, blankets and beads,
and dreams. This house has no dreams. It is a house
with roots that bends with wind and holds.
The earth is a drum and booms with rain
that strikes the taut leather of its face,
and every sound, every whisper of grass
against a horse's flank in Saskatchewan

or the pounding feet of cattle in Wyoming,
that rolls across its strung face booms and calls
down the halls of my house, as you do now,
closing the door behind you and moving in
with your memory of other houses, other seas.

Song for a Beached Whale at White Rock

Chillest of lilies, river clutching its lace hem, oh, whale,
thou art bladderwrack given tongue, thou art salt
given the legs of a hermit crab as waves dream of dominion,
thou art the breath that bares you, breathing your bearing,
the compass in the gull, the spar in the rockfish,
the rigging in the agates spilled across ribbed sand,
smallest bearberry of foam, drenched, delirious,

and before thou wert all, before thou wert green,
before swells, before the larynx channelled between pack ice
and the winds of the stars over the pole,
as green as aphids, between potato fields and fraught
freighters, before we were the samba danced every night
on the silk bedroom of thy tympanum, thou wert the first
angel of the Lord, proud with oysters and loud with mussels,
with fields in your mouth and mountains in your tail
and your children strewn across every stone;
before thou wert, thou wert my prayer.

Thou hath alpine tarns for eyes, thou hath spoken
in rhyme as the waves dreamt of it, thou hath known
the first and the last, the fern of the snail's lust
and the raindrop of the trombone's gloom,
and hath eaten mountains away into canyons, and hath
worn codfish for a necklace on your pearly throat,
neither what is nor what will be, the first snowfall and a man
and a woman entwined in the whitest of sheets.

And now thou art whale and lieth in the naked air
and breatheth the bleak sand, and here,
where people come with buckets and tents
to soothe thee with the sea thou hath breached,
thou weepeth the gulls that rise and scream over cliffs
of sweet peas and cumulonimbus, thy flukes
stilleth with the sweet coal seams of suburban traffic,
thou burieth thyself in a child's plastic beach pail,
thou prayeth that thou shalt become a castle in our hearing,
with moat and battlements crumbling, that the sea,
the mercurial sea, the bowl of the sunset's sulfur and the blue
flame of the wick thou beareth at the base of thy thronging
                                    tongue,
shall wash your keep away. Oh, whale, thou art the more
of thy breath and word what thou art with the softest
susurration of herring in eelgrass, of mackerel passing
by river mouths in the barium night before storm,
and what thou art is all that could be, in the ripples
of thy cedars sweeping the path of the shore. Whale,
thou art not whale. We are whale. Thou art our sea.

Riding My Pretty Little Herrings
into the Mouth of the Moon

You my Chinese box, my Ukrainian doll of iron and mirrors,
you my Baba Yaga full of strawberries and horsewhips,
you my little slip-skinned chapatis I nibble with my fingers,
you chimeras drooling olive oil and plum tomatoes,
I screw open a tin and you are lying there like cigars
in your clotted cream, in your dill, in your brown sugar, in
                                                    your lemon,
oh my alewives in a barrel no thoughts are as sleek as your
                                                    thoughts,
no candor so congressional, no bodies so much
like bright nails dumped from a box into deep harbour,
no nails so charmed, no remembrance so sweetly salt.
I hurl a net of nettles and sinew weighted with pebbles
across the river's mouth; it swishes like rain
as it falls. You fillets of mustard and sweet onions, do you
                                                    hear?
You kippers of salt and cut fingers, do you answer?
You gills of the sea, you cloistered nuns rushing this way and
                                                    that,
laying your rosaries on kelp blotters to straighten your habit
                                                    of prayer;
each leaf is a page from the book that brooks no other,
and you have heard it clamour and know no compromise.
Scallions of the sea, what is a moment among so many?
More! QED. You my tinfoil chakras, you who sparkle
like clothespins on a line being reeled in, you my amour,
my beaches, my mind in a flurry. Oh little salted kippers
dried in the sunshine above the salt hay, little
tinned creamies and bottled blues with pimento hearts,
do you hear what I mouth, here outside the swells,
outside the pickled brine of your baby cukes and black
                                                    pepper?

Darlings, the world that begins and the world that ends have
                                                             ended:
I have the sea in a zinc bucket's moon; I am going to drink it
until it is dry. Come home to me now, you submariners,
you knights and ladies, you my books of hours,
my calligraphed hosannahs; come home while you can,
my elegant pursed lips, my purses of evening eggs.
My desiccated dancers, my little hurricane's daughters,
I spear you and lay you sleeping on the soft white bed of the
                                                  challa bread;
I bring my friends to eat; I lay the sea out like a cloth,
set salt on the table, and lemon, and you, to round out the
                                                         evening,
and such an evening, such a romp shared in glad madness,
my little teeth nipping off your tails and heads;
the oil anointing my fingers, and my friends transcendent.
Herrings, you are resplendent!
Oh, you raging, hoarfrosted, star-whipped tears,
you greased and hooded long-distance stuntmen
who swim through the blue froth of the tankers' wake,
you, my little Gullivers in the Fraser's mouth,
oh, you, my whinnying mares, I will net you!
I will wiggle with you in your bondage. I will mouth the rain
that brings the earth down the long slopes of shale
to the sea, because my eyes are the salt the earth grants up;
when it rains I will dissolve and flow down to you;
you will drink me in a flash and be absolved; the green grass
                                                         will flare
beneath the sinking moon; we will rise up, my pretty ones.
Come, mouth the dance floor of my tongue.
Oh, my shamans, now is our hymnal.
Oh, my hangman's hoods, my weeping, now is our then.
Oh, drooping cedars over the tide's choral, lie thee down
                                                  and rest.
Oh my hearties, oh my worthies, be caressed.
I will sing for you now through the long night, for you have
                                                         always
sung your song for me, your one heartsick song, so plentifully.

Diving for Octopus in Vancouver Port Authority Waters

Eye in a sack, inkpot who hath written
every Rasputin into his dressing room, thou
pearl-fingered kitten, thou brain in a knot,
thou thought with a beak, my sweetest salt and rain,
my drowning tiger, roam now from your rambling
garden of coral, babble of bibles and morals,
of kelp and seasick stars churning in jabble.
My rampage, curl your arms into violas. I would play thee,
but that whispered riddler of roaring, the sea,
sucks my shore away in pebbles and shucks it back in a moan.
It is not rain I wish to have flow through my fingers;
it is not rain that will drop from my lips like bees to a petal;
it is not the sun that will pour out when I split
my tongue to thy beak's bitterest bite and our seas become one:
slyest, thou art mine hand, mine mouth, mine eye.
Thou swimmest in whiskey. Thou breathest gin.
Stars wrap the sands of your nightmare with thine own sheets.
Oh Rubinesque, oh resplendence, repeat after me
your most rueful catarrh: the earth has been raped by regents,
rounded by scoundrels, ripped rib from rib and ripened in a
                                        barrel;
the sea has been gill-netted, purse-seined, bottom rolled,
                        scrolled,
parolled and sieved, stripped of its herring,
carded of its cod, blasphemed out of its holy mackerel,
pumped of its salt, shamed out of swells,
and yet we still love. Despite all recalcitrance,
despite the anger that articulates rhapsody,
we still breathe our first hour, our bodies still flower,
we still become, and the sea we breathe and the air
that breathes us become. Oh, kitten,

the sea has been deboned, dismissed, mapped, anchored
and diked, and still we the rambunctious
on the grey flank of the flood tide, we the recalcitrant
doodles on the blue swells of the river's fiddles,
we the hidden and the forbidden, we who danced first
from the reef to the riddle, from the reed to the bladderwrack,
now at the last, from the deep sea port to the subdivision's infill,
from the salmon to the can and the net-farm's effluent,
from the affluence of sodium streetlight and the freighter's
                                        gargle
to the shoulder of the wooden villages now hidden
behind mountains of sulfur and credulous scoop cranes,
now dance at last, as the band of our memories,
the tubas of praise, the trumpets of sunrise, go down
and all hands are lost as praise is found.

Stirk

Ah, there's one now,
grazing in the field,

a stirk, with flowers
in its teeth

and a year of sun
on its ruddy back. I lean

against a stone fence
and watch a hazel copse

dance with summer
cold that sinks

off purple fells
into the dark

of water, grass,
and rock,

the white house,
the red door, the shock

of arrogance
and settlement.

A woman loved
a man in that house,

brought children
into light and cooked

roots in a black pot
or fought him

to the death that claimed
them both. This is husbandry,

the mud house built
overnight, with smoke

rising in the chimney
before dawn light

to claim common ground
and fence it off

to make it private.
This is love, unseen,

when you strip it down
and the cold

falls from the hills,
a thing that hides

from our earth
and welcomes strangers. The stirk

kicks up his heels
and I am stumped

to say how history
makes us or how

to stand in history
that still is going on

and husbands me
between these fences

balanced rock on rock,
except to walk

across the fields,
lifting gate and latch

and setting them back
as the stirk lifts his head, curious.

You Can't Go Home Again

I ran over a puppy
on the reserve in the dark,

when the stars fell in the rain
and the road breached the rabbit-brush.

In that hot valley the yellow-feathered hills
are folded out of Packards,

the rust so thin a single blade of grass
pushes through them like lovers in a bed

that's just turned into an abandoned
log yard littered with cut glass.

Baby, we're our own intravenous now,
but back then I was just driving home to you,

and the Chevy groaning,
with cutthroat trout drunk on trout flies,

swimming in packed circles
in white honey buckets, smelling of pollen

from Fort St. John. God,
give me the teeth of a bear.

When the puppy ran out of its mind and I clipped it
with my greasy Macpherson struts, Fuck,

before it ran back into the Players cigarette
tin of the abandoned

basketball court razor-wired with knapweed,
my true love, I would have rolled you

between paper fingers and set you alight,
you would have gone up like the little children

in Waco huddling in the cooler with their gingham mothers
stamped out of dough with a rusty tin cutter.

Now the pines are dying. We should not
have loved long enough to see this.

Now the rivers of light drinking the river of rain
flow under our feet in blue flame

and my long trip home is hung out to dry
like whale vertebrae from a five-hundred-year-old

midden, tied up with loose, blue nylon rope
that washed overboard from a trawler

scrawling through the sub pens off Valdez.
Ten years have passed, ten years of words

and children in the dying forests
of the high plateau, yet I'm still in that night

when the puppy ran across the dark road
to bring me home, and I drove on.

Reflections of Soap Lake, WA,
Cast over Chief Joseph and Napoleon
Drinking Coffee in the Window
of the Heaven Café

The road from the Hanford Nuclear Reservation.

The red ochre cliffs above Soap Lake.

The wheels of cars drawing pictographs with ochre dust.

A small bird hiding from the sun with the wind in its beak.

A woman's body floating in the green reflections
of the ochre cliffs across the black volcanic
gravel of the highway dividing the grey wood
town of Soap Lake into the two halves of a Reno Deck.

The lake within the eyes of a man sliding out of a Chevrolet
at the diner in Soap Lake and walking in through crushed
                    Rainier bottles
like a ballet dancer stepping onto a black stage.

The lake within the headlights of the Chevrolet,
blinding the traffic gasping down the road between
the iodine wheatgrass and the dental apparatus of Grand
                    Coulee dam.

The body of Chief Joseph, floating on Soap Lake
with a nylon line and a plug of tobacco,
jigging the Chevrolets nuzzling into the mud.

The white women in their lace cellulite
floating in the starling water like stacked Styrofoam cups.

The coffee grounds of the netted gem fields
on the windswept heights of the Columbia Basin, sprinkled
                                        with salt
drawn from down there by the force within the green flower.

The waitress wiping her sweat in the sun.
The plate of fried eggs drumming its wings against its chest.

The sun living on welfare inside the quarter inch of plate glass
between the coifed waitress and Napoleon bending down
from Heaven to wash his hat in the medicinal pools of Soap
                                        Lake.

The waitress spitting on Napoleon and wiping him off
with a corner of her apron.

The weightless women who don't leave a tip.

Napoleon's hat, as bright as the fender of a Chevrolet
polished with a rag until it gleams like an egg rubbed with oil.

Napoleon with the eyes of a belt buckle
on which a buffalo snorts brass steam.

The cheatweed, the red dust, the strontium.

The sage-green water that gives water wings
to the beautiful women who walk down from their homes
of salt to the midges of Soap Lake.

With one evening on Soap Lake, with one TV in the red room
against the mountain, with no news on any channel,
with only one channel but the desert blinding the hand
in dead roots of sagebrush offering Soap Lake to the sky,

Chief Joseph drinks the waterfall of the sun over the earth
out of a chilled Rainier can, lest it die.

Lest he die breathing the wind that blows over Soap Lake,

lest he just die, candle him;

lay him out in oil: easy him,

lest he die.

The Flea Market

I'm back, with my fold-up table
and my stacks of china (Nippon)

and depression glass, all marked down,
brass elephants missing a tusk, that cookie jar

that's cracked, and wait to see who comes,
who fingers what, who talks, who pays what I ask

(I hide surprise), and who will tell me
what this gadget was when it was used —

you can see it's worn with wear;
you held it here, I think, and placed

your thumb right there, and squeezed,
but for what? Beats me.

It's quite the find. Fifty bucks.
Sometimes collectors come. Sometimes Moms with kids

who wipe their noses with my Irish lace —
I got it at another sale where a woman

was selling Grandma's trunk and all her junk
for a whistle and a song. I bid her down.

The song's to come. We're not the only ones.
The tables stretch from here

to the corner of the parking lot. If it's broken,
junk, out-of-date or in bad taste,

someone has it here, every week
and someone else falls in love

with a book end, a pink glass dish,
can't live without a hair dryer

(hooded) or a gun (pop)
and plunks their money down

to live the life. We all take on
what others have put off.

Hopscotch

We all draw lines, the staggered trail
a man and woman walk through sand,
among broken shells, torn ropes, logs
that slipped from tugs in churning storm,
the chalk that children draw upon the street,
to skip the one square that is death,
to land in Heaven with white clouds,
the curving roof of the cathedral
of house and field, and then return
to cast the stone again to see
where death has moved, for death is not a line,
but what breaks a line and gives it life,

the ribbon stretched around a body
shattered on a curve, around a girl's
bright golden hair, her laughter
that speaks of trust, the wisdom
that the body knows but we, who draw
lines between one word and the rest have
stepped across, the foolish place
that is our only wisdom, where a woman leans,
a man staggers, loses footing,
then walks on.

There are other lines we must cross
or we will break our mother's back.
We hold her hand, but it is hard
to keep up in dread. Only later do we shudder
hard on that crack, knowing that the child
was once that man. These are sacred lines
we hold in trust, unspeakable
crossings made in the dark, when we

become the storm, the sea
that erases lines, breaks ships and casts
spray up to the stars, and turns the cliffs
where we once stood to sand.

The Legendary First and Last Chilcotin Performance of *Peter and the Wolf*

I tip my black hat with the western rattlesnake band
as out on the plateau, west of the Fraser,
between the snow and the name of the snow,
the Tatla Lake School is tuning up for its one-time-only
performance of *Peter and the Wolf.*
You will never see this again. Everyone has come in
from miles around. Moscow is the big bad wolf. Moscow
has one gold tooth.

The German resort owners, the ranchers and big
game outfitters, they've all come
to be dazzled tonight at the turning of the year
back into itself. Moscow! For them, for this one night,
it is a tree with leaves of St. Niklaus,
each with the head of a child — with curls —
while far to the east, unheard in these plywood walls,
some trucker behind on his payments pulls down
the long hill off the plateau to the Fraser, squeak,
a small forest of blue pine stacked up in sections
on his White truck, creak, and south of Alexis Creek
the wild horses that no one has managed to hunt down
yet put their heads into the wind, and tremors
run down their flanks and are blown back, snap.

Right now, everyone forgets all that. Right now,
the drifting reindeer herds of the Russian stars
are pink sugar roses. Some child hits a triangle: ting!
Moscow has all its brittle ting ting ting sparrow
bones folded in its pleated pocket, marked
with the major roads and recipes for bouillabaisse,
because Russia knows all about invasion, *n'est-ce pas?*

and how the only defence is the earth itself.
Here tonight, halfway between the Fraser and the star-sick
Pacific, it is running down those loyal boys in field grey,
who left with their wheat-coloured heads
full of busts of Pindar and Martial and came back
begging for milk. Bwaaaa.

In the Chilcotin, the Milky Way is a bone with a fish's tail.
In the Chilcotin, the Germans still think they belong to the
                                                    earth,
but they learn tonight that the war that is still played
is played with cards of poplar leaves dealt on a table of snow.
Each one is a yellow fish sewn of leather. Each tree
is a house in a distant city. Each stump is a battle. They learn
they are a long way from Moscow now, but, ah,
the band plays on, ding-dong, and the night bends down
with delirious lipstick, and the earth drinks the violin
and cries in strains of grass, *Ruin me!*
as the burnt black hands of the wolves
close in on the throat in the howl, the horse
frozen in the dip of the hummingbird's tongue,
the lover's grimace, the ho in oh, the oh in ho, .
the oh, the I, the eeeee.

Tao Hill

As the waves break on the shush
of gravel, toss up agates under cliffs

that sink into the roots of stories
that have been told since wave

first broke, land heaved, trees
grew from moss by rain-fed streams

and people came from shells,
from dreams, from spells

of anguish and surprise,
moon-mouth rising from black water,

the beach is drawn back out to sea
and roars as each wave speaks.

A woman walks where stone is ground
and herself is blown by rain

and water and turned to salt.
I walk with her. My lips, my tongue,

my hand are all salt now and hear
the rush of pebbles in her fingers, stars

fallen out of dream, not like that other
story, the good man's wife

who looked back. Don't look back.
This is a different story, where only water

tells the words that it would tell
and only water hears its answers

question answers,
and we must tell this story.

ABOUT THE AUTHOR

—

Since 1982, Harold Rhenisch has published ten books and five chapbooks of poetry — lyrical, gnostic, narrative, meditative, mythic, comic, metaphysical, deconstructive and dramatic. He is the English language translator of the German post-modern playwright Stefan Schütz and the editor of *In This Poem I Am: The Selected Poetry of Robin Skelton*. He has published a book of essays, a novel, and four books of creative nonfiction detailing the history and culture of what Patrick Lane has called "the last unknown country" in Canada, the British Columbia Interior, and its place in Canadian and world history. The most recent book in this series, *The Wolves at Evelyn: Journeys Through a Dark Century* (2006), was a finalist for the 2007 Hubert Evans Nonfiction Prize and the winner of the George Ryga Award. An active freelance book reviewer, editor, and teacher, Rhenisch has worked with poets, novelists, essayists and students from British Columbia to Ontario and from Florida to India. A semi-finalist in both poetry and nonfiction in the 2007 CBC Literary Awards, he holds degrees in Creative Writing from the University of Victoria and the University of British Columbia, and has won the Petch Prize, the *Arc* Poem of the Year Award, the Confederation Poets' Prize, the Critic's Desk Award, and the *Malahat Review* Long Poem Prize in both 2005 and 2007. Born in Penticton, B.C., in 1958, he was raised on an orchard in B.C.'s Similkameen Valley, where he worked as a nurseryman, tree grafter and pruner for many years before moving to B.C.'s Cariboo Plateau for fifteen years. He now makes his home in Campbell River, B.C.

MEMBER OF SCABRINI GROUP

Québec, Canada
2007